Cupboard Boy

2

Table of Contents

Prologue

The following is a harrowing story that may be as distressing to read, as it is for me to write. However, the events represented here, which took place during the years 1963 to 1980, need to be recorded for the sake of future generations of children and out of respect to all the children who are suffering, or have already suffered, and perhaps perished, at the hands of demonic parents.

I also hope that the people who are tasked to protect children, whether it be Government agencies, Social Services or teachers and anyone with an ounce of decency, will learn from the experiences of my siblings and myself.

You would think that forty years on child abuse would be a thing of the past. It isn't. Disgustingly, the problem is probably worse now than it ever was back then in the 1960s and 70s.

Child abuse is not just about children being brutally beaten or sexually abused. There are a lot more ways that sadistic and inadequate parents can abuse and destroy a child's life. The list is endless!

At the time of writing, I am fifty-seven, and have served in the Parachute Regiment, the SAS and fought in two wars. During my time in the forces, I witnessed some horrific sights and events, which still haunt me thirty years on.

I now work as a teaching assistant in a secondary school, and sometimes reflect that it's a bit like being back in a war zone. Along with the disruptive and aggressive behaviour and foul language of some of the children, I also see the signs of child abuse on a daily basis. I see children going hungry, their lunch boxes, if they have one at all, containing nothing but a dry slice of bread or a few biscuits. Others come to school wearing clothes that have not been washed for weeks on end. I also see that the kids wearing them are often further abused by their peers, because they smell or are not wearing designer trainers. These children will often rebel and become aggressive and anti-social, while some may become depressed withdraw into themselves.

These days, we are far too quick to blame poor concentration, low achievement and bad behaviour on the fact that the children have Attention Deficit Hyperactivity (ADHD), or Oppositional Defiant Disorder (ODD). These kids are often prescribed stimulants such as Ritalin or Adderall, and the real root causes of their behaviour stemming from parental inadequacy or parental abuse is ignored. Added to this is the fact that many drugs similar in effect to Ritalin or Adderall are addictive, and, in my opinion, may well lead to an addiction to other illegal 'feel-good drugs', such as cannabis and heroin.

A child doesn't have to have a black eye or bruised ribs to be classed as an abused child. Child abuse takes many forms, for example, from not being fed to being over-fed, from being ignored to being screamed at. There are so many ways in which parents can abuse their children, it would take me forever to list them.

Please read this book with an open mind. It has been written to inform and educate rather than entertain.

Dedication

I especially dedicate this book to one hell of a brave boy, my stepbrother, Little Paul, who bore the brunt of the abuse my siblings and I suffered at the hands of demonic parents. Sadly, Paul died at the very young age of 19, and with a great deal of dignity, from cancer.

God bless Him!

The following story is true, although the names of individuals and places have been changed to protect the identity of those concerned.

Chapter One

A Walk in the Dark

I can't remember the exact date, but it was during the winter of 1963, and I was just two and a half years of age. It was a dark, bitterly cold and damp winter evening. The air was still, and thick with the smell of burning coal. Due to the resulting smog, visibility was poor, and I could only see as far as the end of my nose.

I was being pushed along the abandoned streets of a small town in Cheshire. I was in my little pushchair all wrapped up nice and cosy. My mother and I were en route to what was to be our new home, number 62, Hill Street. This was the place where, in the not too distant future, I and my soon-to-be stepbrothers and -sisters would enter into a nightmare existence.

What happened to us, and the things we witnessed between the years 1963 and 1980, would psychologically scar both me and my stepsiblings for life. I know this as a certainty, because even today, at the age of 56, I still receive counselling.

When my mother and I eventually arrived at No. 62, we were greeted by a huge, brick-shithouse of a black man. He was so big that his frame filled the doorframe of the Victorian house, blocking out any light that might have emanated from the inner hallway.

I had never seen a black man before. As he stooped down to greet me, with his huge black face and beaming white smile, I remember feeling quite scared as he towered over me! His breath stank of cigarettes. The memory now plays like a scene from the fairy-tale, Jack in the Beanstalk

The giant also had quite a distinctive, unsightly scar around his right eye, which made him look even scarier. I later learned that the scar was a result of being kicked by a donkey in his teens. I remember some years later, my uncle Allen (his brother), telling some of his friends about the donkey incident. According to him, after the donkey had kicked him, his brother had simply picked himself up off the floor and punched the donkey out cold with a single punch.

This huge guy, who was now leaning over and scaring the crap out of me, went by the name of Roy. He had been born in Jamaica, and was one of many Jamaicans who came to Britain on The Empire Windrush, which famously docked at Tilbury on the

22nd of June, 1948. Roy had originally only intended to stay in the country for a few years, planning to earn a bit of cash and then return to Jamaica. However, Roy fell in love with the U.K., and took a particular liking to British white women.

After the initial shock of meeting such a huge black man for the first time, Roy came across as a nice enough man. Especially after feeding me a few yummy chocolate Dundee biscuits. In fact, it only took an hour or so before he started to grow on me, even though his size still felt quite intimidating, as it still does to this day.

I didn't know it then, but he was going to be my new stepfather. He was also the man I would later hate with a vengeance, and someone I have often dreamt of killing since the age of ten.

I think the only reason I never did attempt to kill him when I was younger, was the fear of the possible repercussions if I failed in my attempt. My fear of failure back then is probably the only reason he is still alive today, despite the fact that I have served with the elite Special Air Service and been trained to kill. Plus, the fact that I am a law-abiding citizen.

Chapter Two

Deserted at Two

My real father, Kenneth, had selfishly deserted my mother and I for another woman about four months prior to this, taking with him my older brother Duncan, aged four, and sister, Caren, aged six.

Mum told me some years later that my father had been having an affair with a woman who lived directly across the road from us. He had been seeing her for several years before moving in with her. In fact, he was seeing the woman at the time of my conception.

Although my dad and his hussy only lived about fifteen yards from us, he never once came back to visit me. Nor did he allow my brother and sister to visit me.

I don't know what went on between Mum and Dad to make him so bitter, but, as far as he was concerned, I didn't exist.

My only memory of my real father prior to him leaving us, was when he rode his motorbike through our front door, which happened to be locked at the time.

According to my mum, he and my mother had fallen out earlier during the day, so whilst he was out at the pub, or with his hussy, Mum put the latch on the door to stop him from coming back in. In his frustration, my dad tried to break the door down with his motorbike. He neither knew nor cared that we kids were playing in the hallway at the time.

Although I was only just over two years of age, I still remember him falling off his motorbike as it crashed through the door, only to stop just short of hitting my sister and me.

His aggression and reckless riding got him into trouble. Within a matter of minutes, some policemen came and took him away, leaving our smashed front door hanging off its hinges.

Later, my uncle Dereck came over to fix it, while my dad had to spend the night at the police station, before appearing before the magistrates the next morning.

A few days later, my father finally abandoned my mother and I, and moved in with his lover across the road, along with Caren and Duncan.

That would not be the last time my father would abandon me over the next few years. In fact, it would be fair to say that he never gave a shit about me, although I have never known why. There was some rumour back then that my mother had also been guilty of playing the field, and that my father may have thought that I was someone else's child?

Anyway, I can't give a shit about him now. Even if I did, it's too late now, as he died when I was 27 without ever speaking to me again.

At the time of his death, I was a soldier and on tour in Northern Ireland. I had just come back from a four-hour street patrol and was tucking into some well-earned scran, when I was called into my troop commander's office and told the news. He'd died of heart failure apparently, which I found ironic, as he never seemed to have one. Not as far as I was concerned!

My commanding officer offered me the opportunity to take compassionate leave so that I could attend his funeral. I declined, deserting my dad for a change.

I think my commanding officer was quite surprised and a little perplexed when I declined his offer of compassionate leave. He probably thought I was in shock. He asked me again the following day, my answer was the same — no.

Chapter Three

Dying for the Loo

It didn't take Mum long to get over my dad leaving her. Within the space of a few months, she had started to enjoy her regular Friday nights out on the town with her girlfriends.

It was whilst she was out on one of those Friday nights that my mother suddenly got caught short, and desperately needed a loo.

As there were no public toilets and no suitable bushes to hide behind in the vicinity, my mother decided to knock on at the nearest house with a light on to ask if she could use their toilet. Unfortunately, the house that she knocked at just happened to be No. 62, Hill Street.

That was the first time that she met Roy – also known as The Obeah Man, which is Jamaican for someone who is evil or practices witchcraft. Mum can have only been in the house for a few minutes, but it was long enough for the Obeah Man to make a memorable impression.

The following day, Mum, nursing a hangover and having a brew with her friend Shirley, recounted her meeting with the black man from No. 62 the previous night. Shirley, who was a bit of a gossip and a nosey cow, quickly realised that Roy was the guy who had lost his wife in a horrible fire a few months previously. It was so shocking that she remembered reading about it in the local weekly broadsheet.

A few weeks later, on another girl's night out, Mum bumped into Roy again, this time in the Express pub. Apparently,

Mum had gone over to him to thank him once again for letting her use his loo. They started chatting and the two of them seemed to hit it off. A few drinks later, they agreed to meet again the following week for a one-on-one date.

A couple of Fridays later, they started to develop a more serious relationship and toyed with the idea of setting up home together. Four months later, Mum and I were moving into this giant of a black man's house.

That was the beginning of my 14-year nightmare.

In the 1960s, the majority of British society did not tolerate mixed-race relationships and racism was rife. Enoch Powell was warning us of the consequences of mass immigration and was building up to his infamous Rivers of Blood speech.

As a result, my mother moving in with a 'black Man' was about as popular as an ashtray on a motorbike. My mum told me that when she first started to date Roy, she would get handwritten letters posted through the door saying stuff like, 'nigger lover', 'white trash' and 'nigger loving whore'. It didn't put her off though, unfortunately.

As far as Mum's mum and dad (my gran and grandad), were concerned, they had only just come to terms with the fact that their daughter couldn't hold on to her husband and was now a divorcee. According to my mum, once, when she turned up in my grandad's local pub accompanied by Roy, Grandad got really upset and a few of his mates threatened to beat the living daylights out of Roy.

The following day, my grandad handed my mum a letter informing her that he and Gran would write her off and never speak to her again if she continued her relationship with Roy. Knowing my grandad, it was probably not as polite as that! Mum ignored them and, true to their word, Nan and Grandad, and the rest of the family, did write her off and send her to Coventry. As a result, I lost them, too. I was left with no brother, no sister, no gran or grandad, no aunts, uncles, or cousins. We were well and truly outcasts.

Chapter Four

The First Night

Number 62 Hill Street was an old, large, damp Victorian three-bed, terraced house. All the rooms had very high ceilings. It seemed massive compared to our own little 1950's council house, and a lot colder and dingier.

The walls were covered in loudly patterned green and white floral wallpaper, which was peeling off in places. There were no carpets on the floors, just cold mosaic tiles or bare floorboards. It didn't have a bathroom and the only loo was outside at the bottom of a narrow yard, which backed on to a huge factory wall that had a few bicycle racks attached to it. If you wanted to pee during the night, it was into a metal bucket kept in the kitchen. The house was in such a state that you would have thought that Roy had only just moved in, but he'd lived there for at least four years — and done absolutely no DIY.

Mum and I had only been there a short time, when I remember him giving me what seemed to be a massive chocolate Dundee biscuit and a carrier bag that contained a little, brightly coloured, tin spinning top. I played with it on the cold floor, whilst my mum and he talked.

Later that evening, a knock at the door led to us being joined by even more black people, both men and women, who all spoke loudly and with accents that I didn't understand. They, too, had very black faces and bright white teeth.

Once again, I began to feel a little scared, as they took turns in looking me over. The men rubbed the top of my head and the women tickled my cheek. All of them had the smell of alcohol and cigarettes on their breath. I remember thinking that I didn't like them being there. They scared me and I wanted to go home!

My selfish Mum didn't take me home. She encouraged me to take a pee in an old steel bucket (our inside loo) before guiding me up a set of creaking wooden stairs, to a dark, dingy and cold bedroom, which had even louder wallpaper than downstairs. The walls were covered in damp patches and the paper was peeling off in places.

Mum stripped me to my underwear, put me into a cold bed and covered me with blanket smelling of damp. She then kissed me on the forehead and said goodnight. As she disappeared through the door, she turned the light out and the room went pitch black dark. Now I was even more scared.

"Mummy! Mummy!" I cried out, wanting her to take me home, but she never returned.

A few minutes later, I heard the sound of loud reggae music emanating from downstairs, and the voices of the people grew louder, too. I wanted to go home to our own quiet, small house, and started to cry myself to sleep.

That night I had my very first reoccurring nightmare.

I dreamt that my bedroom was filling up with giant needles, which were taller than me and around two feet in diameter. Fearing that they would eventually trap me in the room, I started to move them out into the hallway, but every time I removed one from the room, another two would replace it. It seemed as if they were going to suffocate me!

I have had this same nightmare on several occasions since that first night. It wasn't until I was about fourteen that I discovered what triggered the nightmares. It was actually the psychedelic wallpaper in the bedroom. Every time the paper was changed, I would have the nightmare for a few nights until I got used to it. I now only have plain walls in my bedroom!

The following day, I was expecting to go home to our own house. I couldn't wait to get out of No. 62, which looked even worse during the day. I hated the place. It was too big, cold and dirty. I looked forward to getting home.

I waited in anticipation all day. I remember watching my mum's every move, desperately wanting her to unfold my pushchair, put me in it and take me home. Disappointingly, she never went anywhere near the bloody pushchair. We never did go back to our cosy and clean little semi. Instead, my mum once again took me back up to the dark and cold bedroom, for second noise-disturbed night. Again, within minutes of her closing the bedroom door, came the sound of someone knocking at the front door, which was quickly followed by my ears being bombarded with the sound of loud reggae music and strange voices.

A few hours into that second night, my sleep was disturbed by the sound of people arguing loudly and what sounded like glass and furniture being broken. The sounds were very frightening and seemed to go on for ages. Then, I heard the sound of a police car pull up outside. I pulled the curtain to one side and, through the window, saw two police cars, a police van, and as many as eight policemen, all heading to the front door. A few seconds later, I heard the sound of another scuffle breaking out, presumably between the police and Roy's party guests. Eventually, the house fell silent after Roy and two other party guests were manhandled into the back of the black police van. The rest of the partygoers soon went on their way. I later found out that Roy and his two mates had been arrested for hitting a policeman.

I learned through a conversation between Roy and my mother the following day, that the fight had started because one of his mates had tried it on with my mum. Roy got jealous and beat the crap out of him. During the same conversation, I also remember him accusing my mum of leading the fella on and threatening to beat her if she did it again.

After three or four days of being at No. 62, and hoping that every night in that cold dark bedroom would be the last, I finally realised that we weren't ever going to go home, and that I was stuck in this nightmarish existence forever. I remember feeling very sad, frightened and disappointed with my mother for taking me there. I also felt very lonely and missed my brother and sister.

Chapter Five

Caren

After a couple of weeks or so, my sister Caren also came to live with us. I didn't know the reason why she left my dad's. She just appeared one day, suitcase and all.

I remember feeling both excited and sad to see her. On one hand, it was great to have my big sis back, but on the other, I felt sorry for her having to come to this scary and horrible place with this horrible man.

Caren had always been a great sister. She always seemed to be there for me. I remember her feeding me from time to time, and rocking me to sleep in my pushchair when I was a baby. I had truly missed her over the last few months.

She gave me a great big hug, and I remember not wanting her to let me go. I also remember thinking that her hug was the first hug that I had received in over six months. My mum never hugged me and I definitely didn't want Roy to hug me. He might have crushed me with his huge arms.

Once Caren had unpacked and settled in, we both went to her bedroom to play. Caren had a little tin, toy cooker, with tiny pots and pans, which we would play with together for hours, inventing different meals. We even made food lookalikes from coloured putty. I was happy then, in our little family unit. Once Caren arrived, I even grew less frightened of dark, because I knew she was there to protect me!

Apart from the noise from Roy's regular party nights, and the fact that the whole of my mum's family and friends had sent us to Coventry, we were probably leading a fairly normal life. I still missed my brother Duncan, though.

Then, one day, some two or three months after Big Sis came back into my life, my world fell apart once again.

I went into my sister's bedroom to find her on the bed curled up in the foetal position. She was crying almost uncontrollably. I remember asking her what was wrong. She didn't say anything, but just grabbed me and gave me the biggest, tightest hug ever. I asked her several times more why she was crying, but she never replied, only holding me tighter and sobbing even more. I didn't like my sister crying and felt so sad for her. Worried and frightened, I also started to cry, until I eventually fell asleep in her arms for what seemed like an age, although it was probably only for half an hour in reality.

Someone knocking and banging on the front door woke me. Shocked and scared once more, I clung to Caren. Then, I heard Roy having a heated argument with another man. They were shouting so loudly and threatening each other that it scared me even more. Once again, I hugged Caren, this time even tighter. Caren gently pushed me away, held me at arm's length and just stared at me with sad, tear-glazed eyes.

I didn't know what was about to happen, but I knew in my heart that things were about to change, and probably not for the better.

Then after a few minutes, the arguing voices quietened a little, as if to allow my mum to speak. Then, Mum called up the stairs.

"Caren, say goodbye to your brother and come downstairs."

"Your dad is here to collect you."

Collect her! Where is she going? I wondered, with dread in my heart. Then, I realised who was at the door — *my Dad.* My heart skipped a beat. I looked at Caren excitedly.

"Dad's here. He's come to take us home," I said, with a broad smile spreading across my face, as I tried to hug her once more. Again, she gently resisted the hug and stared into my eyes. As I looked into them, all I could see were tears and sadness.

"Dad's here, Caren," I repeated, hoping it would cheer her up. It didn't. She kissed me on my forehead.

"Stay in the room. I'll see you soon," she said, tearfully. Then, she disappeared through the bedroom door, her suitcase in hand.

I remember feeling very confused. *Here was my dad, my real dad. So, why wasn't she happy? And why should I have to stay in my room? He's my dad, too.*

I hadn't seen my dad for what seemed like a lifetime, and had little recollection of what he looked like. So, I made my way to the child- gate at the top of the stairs. I got there just in time to see my big sister exiting through the front door, and out of my life forever. As she shut the door, my Mum looked at me. She seemed to have sad eyes, too.

I rushed back into my room to peer through the window that looked down onto the street. I was just in time to see my dad's grey Austin A40 drive off. I remember thinking at the time, *why didn't my dad want to see me, too? Where is he taking Caren, and why aren't I going with them?*

That was the first time I remember feeling deep and almost painful sorrow, the kind that weighs heavily on the heart and can scar your mind forever. I ran back to my room and started to sob my little heart out. I didn't want to be there. I wanted my sister, my brother, my dad and our house back.

Eventually, my mum came up, supposedly to comfort me. I asked her where Caren had gone. She told me that Caren no longer wanted to live with us, and that she would now live with my dad and my brother. I remember asking if she would ever come back.

"Maybe one day," she replied, then gave me a long hug, whilst trying to hide the tears in her own eyes. I really believe that, at that moment, she also wished that she could go home. We couldn't, though. My mum had given up our little council house and her family had written us off. We were trapped!

The long hug my mum gave me that day, was the last hug she ever gave me.

It still hurts me today when I recall the heart-wrenching sadness I felt for days after losing my sister, my best and only friend. I also felt very hurt that my dad hadn't even said hello, let alone taken me along with my sister. I wondered why not, feeling, even at such a young age, very betrayed by someone who should have been there for me, protected me and, above all, loved me — my dad!

A few years down the line, my dad's brother, Uncle Ron, and his wife and my three cousins visited us. They were about to emigrate to Australia on the £10 POM Scheme, and wanted to say goodbye to me and my mum before they left. I learned from a conversation that I heard that day, between my mother and uncle, that the reason my real dad came and took Caren away was because Roy had severely beaten her one day across the legs. Caren had told her primary school teacher, who then called my real dad, who took my sister back into his home. I remember thinking, *why remove one of your children from a violent home, and leave the other, the youngest, to suffer? How sick is that?* I still ask myself that question today.

As my life changed over the next thirteen years, the hurt and the incredible sadness that I felt the day my father took my sister away and left me behind, turned into an increasing hatred for him. He died at the age of 66 without us ever meeting again, and without my forgiveness.

Chapter Six

New Year's Eve 1964

A few months after Caren's departure, things started to get back to normal. Life didn't seem too bad, and I was getting used to living at No. 62 with Roy and my mum. I even got used the parties they often threw. Our house always seemed to be full of people playing loud music and drinking well into the early hours.

It was on one such night, New Year's Eve, 1964, after the party guests had gone, that I was woken by the sound of my mother and Roy screaming at each other. Roy was accusing my mother of flirting with one of the partygoers, and threatening to kill her if she ever dared to cheat on him. Then, I heard my mum scream even louder, as he started to beat her up on the staircase. I could hear the dull thud of each blow, as Roy's fist connected to my mum's face. I will never forget the sound.

My mother begged him to stop hitting her, but the more she pleaded, the more the blows fell. Finally, the house went scarily silent. At first, I thought the silence meant that he had killed her.

I was so scared that he would turn his anger on me. I was hiding under the bed, when my mother came into my room a few minutes later, whimpering and with tears running down her battered, bruised and bloodied face. It was horrible, and I felt dreadfully sick at the sight of her battered face.

She hurriedly got me dressed, took me downstairs. Then, once again, my mum and I were walking the dark, cold and foggy streets of Cheshire, with her still whimpering in pain.

After walking the streets for what seemed like hours, we eventually arrived at my nan's house. She didn't seem too pleased to see us in the early hours of the morning, and made that very clear. At first, she seemed quite reluctant to let us in, although she did in the end. I think she probably felt sorrier for me than my poor, battered mother.

After a quick glass of milk, Nan laid me on her sofa in the front room and covered me with a blanket. There was no kiss on the cheek though, just a simple, "go to sleep now." She and my mum then went into the back room to talk. Actually, they argued rather than talked. I heard Nan telling my mum that she knew it would come to this. She also reminded Mum that she had been warned, and now that she had made her bed, she must lie in it!

I didn't sleep well that night. The sofa was uncomfortable, and I couldn't get the sound of Roy beating my mother up, and her begging him to stop, out of my head. Nor could I shake off the image of my mum's wrecked face.

The following day, I woke up feeling relieved to be at my nan's and no longer having to live with Roy, the man who beat my mum and scared the crap out of me. Nan's was a safe place, a happy place, and it felt good seeing my lovely grandad again. I had missed him.

Later that day, whilst I was drawing trains with my grandad, Roy came knocking at the front door. Nan answered the door. Grandad, my mum and I could hear Nan giving him what for, telling him to go back to the hole he had crawled from. She had a right go at him.

Eventually, my mum joined my nan at the front door and, after a few minutes, I heard Nan shout a few expletives before banging the door shut.

When Nan returned to the back room, she was furious and shaking with anger, her face the colour of beetroot. She was angry that my mum had decided to join Roy outside for a 'private chat'. Roy wasn't allowed in Nan's house, ever. Neither she nor my grandad liked black people, especially those who beat their daughter to a pulp.

After about fifteen minutes or so, my mum came back in and informed my nan that she was giving Roy one more chance. We were going back to No. 62.

My heart sank at the news. I instantly began to panic. I could feel my little heart beating rapidly, and I started to sweat. I didn't know it then, but now I'm sure I had a panic attack.

Nan wasn't very happy about it either. I remember her yelling at my mum not to come back to her house, as long as she was with him. Actually, I think it went more like, 'don't even think about coming back, as long as you're with that black b......!', as Roy drove off.

By teatime that evening, I was back at No. 62 and in my cold and dingy bedroom. I remember looking at the sky and watching clouds as they passed by so slowly, wishing I could be somewhere else. Anywhere else but here!

That New Year's Eve in 1964 would not be the last time that Roy would beat my mother over the next twenty years that they were together. In fact, she got a good kicking every New Year's Eve that I can remember!

On 23rd of December, 1965, whilst I was at Chester Zoo with a friend of my mum's, my mum gave birth in our front room to my first half-sister Jane. It was funny seeing her for the first time. She was still quite wrinkly and her head was a funny shape. She was also neither white nor black, she was more a light brown. I remember asking my mum why she was a different colour from her and Roy. She said it was because there was a bit of Roy and herself in Jane, smiling as if she were proud of the fact, she had created a new life with a horrible woman beater.

Having said that, it was nice having a baby sister around the house. I enjoyed helping my mum look after her. I still have fond memories of rocking her to sleep in her big silver cross pram in the dining room. I was allowed to feed her sometimes, too.

Life continued to be relatively normal for a while. I started primary school and really enjoyed mixing and playing with the other kids. What I liked most of all though was the school dinners. The food always tasted fab. I especially loved the jam and cornflake tart with custard.

However, my time at primary school was also the time when I first became aware of racial prejudice. I was in the playground at the end of the day waiting for my mum to pick me up, when I overheard a couple of the other mums talking to each other.

"Here comes the one with the chocolate kid," said one, pointing in the direction of my approaching mother and half-sister Jane.

Even though I was only four, coming on five, years of age, I knew she was being negative and disrespectful. I remember that was the first time that had made me feel embarrassed about having a mixed-race sister and a black step-dad. That feeling of embarrassment stayed with me for the whole of my childhood.

Chapter Seven

Stanley and Ella (then there were four)

I was six and in the last year of infant school. Life was fairly good, apart from the increasing racial abuse, which now came, from not only the parents, but the children, too. If they were annoyed or upset with me, they would repeat things that I knew they had heard from their parents. I recall one lad getting upset with me because I scored a goal when we were playing football. I called him a bad loser.

"At least my mum's not a nigger lover," he replied, using a phrase he must have overheard somewhere. Probably at home. It was tough at times, but I never let it get the better of me. Not in primary school anyway. Racism aside, I was reasonably happy there, from what I remember.

Then, one day I arrived home from school to find our dining table loaded with food. There were fairy cakes, sandwiches, sausage rolls and, of course, my favourite chocolate Dundee biscuits. I asked my mother why all the food was on the table.

"We have some visitors coming for tea," she replied.

"Is it Caren and Duncan?" I asked excitedly.

"You'll have to wait and see," Mum replied, with a smile.

I spent the next hour feeling so excited, believing that my brother and sister were coming to visit me, I could hardly contain myself.

When Roy finally arrived back home accompanied by our visitors, I was devastated when I realised it wasn't Duncan and Caren at all. Instead, it was a couple of mixed-race kids the same colour as Jane.

Roy introduced them as Ella and Stanley, Ella was aged eight and Stanley almost six.

"Who are they, and why are they here?" I remember asking quite bluntly. Mum looked toward Roy, who explained that they were his children, and that they had been staying with relatives for the last few years.

I wondered why they didn't live with Roy, and why they had just suddenly shown up out of the blue. But I never bothered asking. I was so disappointed that they weren't Caren and Duncan, I didn't care. I consoled myself by busily tucking into the grub.

After we had eaten, Roy and my mum suggested that we kids' go upstairs and play, whilst they talked. Stanley seemed okay, but I didn't really get on too well with Ella, who came across as a bit sly and not a very nice person. She also seemed to have issues with my mother, my little stepsister and me. I noticed her giving my mum and sister the evil eye on more than one occasion. She generally wasn't very friendly at all. I later came to understand the reason for her dislike of the three of us, once I learned what had happened to her own mother.

Her Mum had been standing next to an open fire in her nightdress and dressing gown, when a rogue flame set her clothing alight. She panicked and ran out onto the street, fully ablaze. Neighbours tried to put out the flames that engulfed her, but to no avail. The poor woman died there and then, right outside No. 62, in full view of her kids.

To top it all for Ella, her so-called father had, within a few months of her mother's death, farmed out all the kids to various foster and care homes, and moved my mum and me in. She had good reason not to like us.

Although Stanley and I did get on fairly well throughout the evening, I do recall wishing that they would just go back to where they came from.

I asked my mother several times that evening what time they were going. She never once replied. Eventually, I asked Roy.

"They are your new brother and sister, and they are here to stay," he said with a broad smile on his face.

I wasn't too keen on that idea, as it meant not only sharing a room with Stanley and Ella, but sharing a bed top-to-tail with them, too, as there was only one bed. Caren's old single bed in the box room had been replaced by Jane's cot. The thought of sharing a bed with two strangers filled me with dread. However, there was nothing I could do about it. I was just a six-year-old and had no say in the matter.

I remember the first night we shared the creaky, old, metal- framed bed. Ella was in the middle, head at the top, and Stanley and I were on either side, heads at the bottom. It was a tight squeeze and every time one of us moved, the squeaking bed woke us all up. Stanley also wet the bed for the first couple of nights.

The sheets were taken off and dried on the line every day, but not washed. So, after a few days, our bed stank.

We probably didn't smell so sweet, either. In those days, we kids only had a bath once a week, and that was in either Roy's or my mum's used water.

It took a while, and there were the inevitable squabbles over the sleeping arrangements, Stanley peeing the bed and toy sharing etc., but the three of us eventually learned to get along. A few months down the line, Roy and my mum were given three second-hand beds and mattresses from somewhere, so that we all had our own beds. Ella moved into the box room with Jane. This helped improve our sibling relationship immensely. As we became closer over the next year or so, Stanley gradually began to replace the brother that I hadn't seen since the day my real dad walked out. However, like all brothers, we did fall out with each other from time to time.

On one occasion, when we were seven-and-a-bit years old, Stanley and I had quite a vicious argument. He was trying to blackmail me into stealing sweets from our local shop, over an incident that had happened at school. I refused, which led us to start fighting.

Roy broke the fight up, and then the strangest thing happened; as he did so, he whacked Stanley on the backside with such ferocity that his legs left the floor. It was quite frightening to see, especially because I was expecting to get it next. But, instead of giving me a similar whack, he simply looked at me and ordered me to go to my bedroom. I wasn't going to hang around. I was so scared I ran up the stairs and

Sat between the beds, worried that he might come up and start beating me, too.

He didn't. He just carried on ranting and raving at Stanley and Ella about how they had to learn to get on with each other. I also heard him use the F-word several times. I remember being confused about the fact that Roy had punished Stanley and not me. Did he feel that he had more right to punish his own kids or had the brush with my dad over his beating of Caren have an influence? I eventually fell asleep between the two beds, only awakening when my mother came to put me to bed.

"What about tea?" I asked. She flippantly replied that there was no tea tonight, as naughty children didn't get fed. I remember feeling very shocked at what she said. It was as if a stranger had replaced my mother.

I never slept a wink that night. I was starving hungry and I couldn't get the fact that Roy had punished Stanley and not me out of my head. Somehow it didn't seem fair.

That was the first time, but certainly not the last, that I and my stepsiblings were sent to bed without food. That was also the day we all started our journey into hell. The fight between Stanley and I had somehow flipped Roy's switch. From there on in, every little misdemeanour would have a heavy physical price to pay— the Belt.

There was one time when Ella had been playing up my mum. I think she had refused to do the washing up, or take out the rubbish. Anyway, they fell out, and Mum used the dreaded six words for the first time, the words that would put the fear of God into all of us for the rest of our childhood;

"Wait until your father comes home."

Whenever those words were uttered, it always resulted in one or all of us getting a brutal beating, followed by long, hungry nights in bed.

That particular night, Roy came home while we kids were all upstairs in our rooms. I heard my mother telling him how badly behaved Ella had been, and how she was sick of the way she behaved toward her, not respecting her, and so on. Mum said that Roy needed to teach Ella a lesson, or she and I would leave.

A few minutes later, Roy came to the bottom of the stairs and called for Ella to come down. Stanley and I looked at each other, both of us completely shocked at what my mum had told Roy. By this time, we were both aware of what Roy was capable of, especially after a few drinks, and were genuinely scared for Ella. A few minutes later, we were both shocked at the chilling sounds that came from downstairs. As long as I live, I'll never forget the sound of Roy's thick, wide leather belt as it connected with the bare skin of Ella's backside, nor her screams of agony, as she begged him to stop with every lash. Her ordeal went on for a good five minutes.

Ella later told Stanley and I that Roy had made her take her knickers off and told her to lie on the sofa, whilst he whacked her at least twelve times, while ranting, raving and occasionally laughing at her, as she squirmed and wriggled in pain. We didn't know it then, but the sound of leather pounding on bare skin was about to become very familiar to us over the next ten years.

Chapter Eight

He Counted the Bread Slices

As kids, we were often guilty of tiny misdemeanours, either breaking things accidentally, or just being argumentative with each other. I used to fall out with Ella quite a lot, as she was always suspected of telling on Stanley and me.

These slip-ups gave Roy or my mum an excuse to either whack us, or send us to bed with no food. The nights without food punishment was usually handed out by my mother, while the whacking was Roy's speciality.

On the second of two nights in a row that we had been sent to bed without food by my mother, Stanley and I, unable to sleep because of the hunger, waited until everyone was asleep and snuck downstairs to make ourselves some sugar butties. Being the age, we were, and unaccomplished at making butties, we obviously left a few clues, like leaving spilt sugar and forgetting to put the butter away.

The following afternoon when I got home from school, Roy asked me if I, or anyone else, had been downstairs during the night. Fearing the belt, I lied, saying no, I didn't think so, which he seemed to believe at the time.

It soon became obvious that he didn't. A few nights later, we were hungry once more. Again, we waited until we were sure Roy and Mum were asleep. This time though, all three of us, Ella, Stanley and I, helped ourselves to sugar butties. This time we were extra careful, and ensured that we cleaned up afterwards.

The next afternoon, when Roy came home from work at three o'clock, he called us all downstairs. When we were all present, he told us all to take our pants down and face the wall in the living room. *I don't know why he insisted on us taking our pants down before whacking us. He probably liked to see the welts he was making on our young skin, the sick bastard! None of us had a clue as to why we were about to be beaten.* However, we all did as we were told. As I looked at the wall, from the corner of my eye, I could see Stanley and Ella to the left of me. They looked terrified. Stanley was so scared about what was to come that he actually wet himself a little, and all three of us were shaking with fear, as we heard Roy removing the long, wide leather belt from around his waist.

He walked up to Stanley first.

"Have you been stealing food?" he asked. Stanley must have turned his head to speak.

"Don't turn around," Roy shouted, as he smashed Stanley's face against the wall, causing his nose to bleed. He then whacked Stanley with the belt. He asked again. "Have you been stealing food?"

"No, Dad," Stanley lied.

Whack!

"You're fucking lying. I hate liars. Tell me the fucking truth."

"No, Dad, honest."

Whack! Whack!

"Okay, you think you're smart," said Roy. "I'll come back to you in a minute, you little fucking thief." He moved up the line to Ella.

Whack!

"Have you been stealing food?" he asked her.

"No, Dad."

Whack, whack, and whack!

"You're fucking lying. Have you been stealing food, you little bitch?"

"No, Dad, honest, I haven't done anything," pleaded Ella.

Whack, whack, whack!

"Liar!"

Whack!

I quickly realised that Roy was getting angrier at every swing of his belt. He'd gone from whacking Stanley once after every question, to whacking Ella twice or three times after each question. By the time he got to me, I had already wet myself with fear. I had heard Stanley and Ella being beaten before, but up to this point; I had never been beaten with the belt myself. That was something that I had often felt guilty and embarrassed about. All I'd ever received until now was a smack on the arse or a crack around the head. Roy had never really gone to town on me. I think it was because of his assault on Caren, and the fact that he had been caught out by the school and my real dad. That had held him back from giving me as severe a beating as the others. I also think that he thought it was somehow more acceptable to beat his own black kids than a white step-kid.

I remember shaking uncontrollably as I waited for my first ever whack of the belt. he stood behind me.

Whack

"Paul," he asked me, "have you been stealing food?"

'No Dad'

Whack, Whack.

"Yes, Dad," I replied, peeing myself a little more with fear.

Whack! There was a short pause.

"What did you just say?" Roy asked, obviously not quite believing his ears.

"Yes, Dad, I stole some bread and sugar," I said, ready for the next whack.

'Who else?' He asked.

'Just Me Dad' I said, trying to protect my siblings from another belting.

There was another pause whilst I waited for the next blow, but the next blow never came. Instead of hitting me again, he started ranting on about there being at least one thief who was honest enough to admit to stealing. He then gave me one last whack, before sending me off to my room. Needless to say, I didn't hang around. I didn't even stop to pull my wet pants up!

Even though I had personally escaped any more violence that night, I couldn't escape the horrific sounds of the further beatings. Nor could I escape hearing the cries of Stanley and Ella, as he continued to beat them, calling them, 'dirty, fucking liars. I remember desperately wanting them to admit to their crime, just to end the beating. I cried myself to sleep that night, not because I was in pain, because I was. I cried for Stanley and Ella, as I heard them crying and begging for mercy, while Roy beat them relentlessly.

Stanley and Ella never came up to their rooms that night. Roy made them stand with their arms outstretched and touching the wall all night. If they moved, he would whack them with the belt.

They never did confess to stealing.

Later in life, whilst I was undergoing SAS interrogation training, I was made to adopt that position for four hours, and I can tell you that it was bloody tough going. God knows what it must have been like for Stanley and Ella, who were so young and small.

The following day, I was the only one of us children to go to school. Roy had beaten Stanley and Ella so badly that they were unable to walk properly. Also, if they had gone to school, someone might have reported their injuries to Social Services, who would most certainly have reported it to the police. That kind of attention was something child abusers like my mum and Roy avoided like the plague.

As I was about to leave for that day for school, my mum gave me a folded-up note to give to Stanley's teacher. I read it on the way. It said, 'Stanley cannot attend school for the next few days, due to him catching Chicken Pox.' We all had quite a lot of ailments that would keep us off school over the next few years. Off the top of my head, we had chicken pox three times and measles at least twice, as the beatings became both more severe and frequent. We were punished for any minor misdemeanour.

I remember giving the letter to the stuck-up school secretary, and her reading it before throwing it in the bin and dismissing me with a wave of her scrawny hand. I wanted so much to tell her that the note was a lie, and that the real reason Stanley wasn't at school was because he had been beaten black and blue. But I got the impression that she wouldn't have given a crap. Plus, I was afraid of the beating I might get when I got home.

Roy worked shifts, 6 a.m. to 2 p.m. and 2 p.m. to 10 p.m., as well as nights. We kids always used to look forward to him going to work, especially if he was on the night shift, or the 6 -2 shift, but we dreaded him being on the 2 - 10 shift. This was because, if one of us were due a beating during that week, it would always be twice as savage, as Roy had usually had a drink or two before coming home and dishing out the punishment.

I often watched the clock at around the time he was either going to work, or about to come home, dreading the latter.

The beatings became less frequent after about a year or so, as we learned to toe the Roy line. The fear that they could always come back at any time also kept us all on our toes and in check.

Chapter Nine

Burley Street (the move)

Just after I turned eight, we moved less than five-hundred yards from our run-down Victorian house on Hill Street, to a more modern house, No. 27, Burley Street.

We children had no idea we were moving. We were picked up from school by Mum at half-past three, and then taken straight to the new house. On the way, we walked past No. 62, where I noticed that the windows were boarded up and an A4 sheet of paper was taped to the front door. I remember wondering why that was, although I never asked. Sometime later, I found out that we had actually been evicted for non-payment of rent.

The new house was a council house. It was okay, a bit smaller than Hill Street, but at least it had a bathroom and an inside toilet. No more peeing in a bucket or bathing once a week in a tin bath. It even had central heating with radiators in all the rooms. Bliss! Well, it would have been bliss, if Roy had ever allowed Mum to put the central heating on. The only form of heating he would allow was from the gas fire in the lounge and only when he was in occupancy.

Outside, there was a flagged yard for a garden, at the bottom of which were two concrete buildings. One was a shed. The other, slightly smaller building, was the now disused coal bunker, which had metal doors on top and a small, metal drop-down hatch which would have been used for accessing the coal.

Our new next-door neighbours on one side were the Ashby's, who had three boys, Ken, James and Peter. Their mum was Paula, and she and my mum seemed to get on very well, as did we kids.

On the other side of us was a widow by the name of Kath. She was a lovely old lady, who used to bake lots of cakes and scones. Occasionally, she'd pass some over the wall to us, and we would sometimes get to eat them, if Roy wasn't about. If he were, he would make us put them in the cake tin that my mum kept on a high shelf in the kitchen. Then, they would never be seen again. Not by us kids, anyway.

The gate at the bottom of the yard faced the long, tall brick wall of a church garden. On the other side of the wall were the Vicar's children, Jenny and Dave. They both spoke with very posh accents and wore smart clothes, as they looked down on us from their raised garden. They seemed nice enough, though. The church and the rectory were due to be demolished about a month or so after we moved in, so the Vicar's family were moving to a new church down South somewhere. Before they left, they passed many of their old toys over the wall to us. Amongst them were a number of board games, colouring pencils and a calligraphy set, which I claimed and wrote with for hours on end.

The friendship with the 'church kids' was short, but very memorable. The contrast between our two families was like a pebble to a mountain. I don't need to tell you who the pebbles were!

The fact that we didn't have a large garden didn't matter to us. We still had lots of fun playing with our new friends next door. We played football, cricket, occasionally hopscotch, as well as the board games that Jenny and Dave had given us. Life definitely improved for us kids during the first few months of moving to Burley Street. Even Roy seemed to be more relaxed, treating us to a day out to Rhyl in North Wales, though I think it that was more for his benefit than ours.

I remember there was a little fair near to the beach. We were all given a sixpence each for spending money, which was barely enough for a ride on one of the attractions. Personally, I didn't care. I had never been to the seaside and loved watching the sea and hearing the sound of the waves crashing into the prom wall.

I don't ever remember feeling really happy during childhood years. But, if I was, it was on that hot summers day looking out at the sea.

On the way back, we stopped off at a pub, where Roy bought us two bottles of coke and two packs of crisps. We shared them between the four of us, as we sat at the picnic tables outside. Mum and Roy on the other-hand had a posh pub meal inside. They kept us waiting in the hot sun for nearly two hours, whilst the inconsiderate bastards scoffed their roast dinner.

By the time we got home at eight o'clock that evening, it was decided by Roy that it was too close to bedtime to eat, even though us kids had only eaten a half bag of crisps the whole day. He sent us to bed hungry.

Chapter Ten

No Ball Games

One day, we and the Ashby kids were in our yard playing cricket and having a great time, when Ken from next door got a bit frustrated and bowled the ball a little too hard. It deflected off my bat and smashed through the dining room window of our house. My mum went berserk. She made the Ashby's go back to their own yard and all of us had to come in and go to our bedrooms. She then had an argument and fell out with Paula next door, even though Paula had promised to pay for fixing the window, because Ken had admitted bowling the ball in frustration. To be honest, though, I think my mum was more worried about how Roy would react, rather than who would pay for the window.

Stanley, Ella and I knew there would be a price to pay when Roy got home from work. The fact he was on a 2 - 10 shift, and would probably be half cut whilst punishing us, would make it worse. The beatings were definitely more ferocious once he'd had a drink, which made us worry more. I can remember lying awake in my bed dreading the moment he would return. Every car door that slammed shut unnerved me more.

I don't know exactly what time he eventually rolled in, although it seemed later than usual. I could hear him ranting and raving about the 'fucking useless bastards of kids'. My fear level rose with every rant, as he sounded more pissed than usual.

Luckily, for all our sakes, he never came up that night. Instead, he took it out on my mother and gave her a good thumping, something he usually reserved for the early hours of New Year's Day, or when he couldn't get hold of any weed. Which he smoked almost continuously.

He only ever took my mum out on New Year's Eve, and for some reason or other, every year without fail, he would beat the crap out of her when they got home. I think it was because she never went out at any other time of the year, and made up for that on the one night she was able to. She probably made Roy jealous when she flirted with other men, or vice-versa.

I know it probably sounds terrible, but I was somewhat glad that she got it that night. After all, her getting the beating meant that we didn't. I still never got any sleep, though. Just the fear that he might decide to change his mind and sort us out that night kept me awake.

The next morning, my mum's face was a right state. He must have really gone to town on her. Both of her eyes were black and her top lip was as swollen as a well-fed leech.

When Roy eventually surfaced at mid-day, he lined us all up again and started ranting, telling us we were, 'little fucking useless bastards.' He also said that there were to be no more ball games in the yard and that we were no longer allowed to play or talk with the neighbours.

I think the thought of not being able to play with the kids next door hurt more than any beating we might have got.

Then, we were sent outside to play, whilst he and my mum went upstairs, 'to make up'.

When I got outside, I saw in the corner of the yard our two footballs, which had been burst, as well as the cricket bat that had been broken in half. The bastard had even cut the tennis balls in half.

We didn't speak to the neighbours for about two weeks. After which, we were all back in and out of each other's yards. Obviously, we were in their yard more often than not, especially when Roy was at home. At least we could play ball games there.

Chapter Eleven

Lara

On November 5th of 1971, my mum gave birth
to another half-sister, Lara. I remember the night well.
Once my mum started to go into labour, Stanley, Ella
and I were banished to the rear yard, to watch other
people's firework displays. It was great at first,
watching the spectacular fireworks. I remember
looking up to the sky, amazed at the beautiful colours
and patterns they made.

A few hours later, after the fireworks had
finished, the three of us began to get very cold. Even
though we complained of our coldness several times,
we were not allowed back into the house until the
baby was born, at 10.15 p.m. that night.

The poor girl, I remember thinking at the time. We had started to dislike and despise her before she had even been born, thanks to our inconsiderate bastard of a father, who, by the way, was half pissed and high on cannabis by the time Lara arrived.

"A quick look at the baby and straight to bed," Mum said, as we entered the front room where our new sister, and Mum and Roy's next potential victim, lay so innocently in her Moses basket.

"Can we have something to eat first mum?" Stanley asked.

"It's too late at night to be eating, it will give you nightmares," she replied, apparently without a care in the world.

What could be worse than the nightmare we're already living in? Great, I remember thinking, *another restless night, with my stomach yearning to be filled.*

Hunger is a horrible sensation. I can't begin to imagine how the children of starving nations must feel. Even now, at the age of 56, I can't sleep unless I know there is food readily available to eat.

My old job frequently required me to stay overnight in hotels. My biggest fear was not sleeping in a strange place like most other people, but that the vending machines would be out of order!

After Lara was born, the beatings seemed to phase out again. The punishment handed out for naughty behaviour was simply a good bollocking and hungry nights in bed. That didn't last long though!

Chapter Twelve

Little Paul (makes six)

About three or four months after Lara was born, Stanley, Ella and I arrived home from school to find the dining room table loaded with yummy food once again.

Stanley and Ella started to speculate as to the reason for such a sumptuous spread.

"Is it someone's birthday, or is Mum pregnant again?" Stanley wondered. I, on the other hand, had seen it all before, on the day that they, Stanley and Ella, had arrived on the scene. *That's all we need, more kids! Where are they all going to sleep? The place is cramped enough already,* I remember thinking. We only had three bedrooms. I hoped it would be a girl, or girls. At least then Stanley and I wouldn't have to give up our precious space in the box room.

We had to wait nearly four hours for our visitor to turn up. The wait was excruciating. I could see the yummy food, and I was absolutely famished. However, we weren't allowed even a morsel until our visitor arrived. As time wore on, I began to panic. *What if he comes too late for us to eat? Will we have to go to bed hungry again?* I desperately hoped not.

At exactly 8.30 p.m. that evening, a woman from Social Services delivered our new brother. He was mixed race, like Ella and Stanley, and was called Paul. We were quickly introduced to him, and then finally let loose on the food, which we devoured with gusto.

I now believe that Roy and my mum put on such lavish spreads to lull Social Services, and us kids, into a false sense of security. It was too much of a coincidence to be anything else.

Paul was eighteen months my junior, but was actually taller than me. He seemed a nice enough boy, and I must admit I liked him instantly. He was a funny little chap, a wee bit cheeky in a harmless way. Although Roy was his biological father, he had a different mother to Stanley and Ella.

I would find out later that Roy was a prolific cheater, and had sired kids all over the place, with many different women.

Paul was the result of a relationship that Roy had had with another woman, named Sheila. Their affair took place whilst he was married to Stanley and

Ella's mum. Paul's mother, feeling abandoned by Roy after he chose to stay with his wife, had handed Little Paul over to Social Services, stating that she couldn't cope. Paul was placed with foster parents, who had looked after him for the last two years.

Once we had eaten our tea, the problem with names was discussed. The new Paul was younger than me, so it was decided that he would be known as Little Paul, and I would be known as Big Paul.

The first night that Little Paul joined the family, he had to top- and-tail with Stanley, until Roy and Mum could get him his own bed. When we were alone in our, now very cramped, bedroom, Little Paul started to ask some very uncomfortable questions.

" Do you always eat lovely food like that?", and, "Isn't Dad nice?" he asked. Obviously, he was excited about gaining a whole new family after living for the last few years as the only child with a pair of older foster parents.

Not wanting to burst his bubble, I stayed silent. I had only just met him, and was afraid that anything I told the interloper might, accidentally or otherwise, get back to Roy.

If he only knew what lies ahead for him, he would have begged to stay with his aged foster parents, I thought, as I closed my eyes in an attempt to get some sleep. I didn't sleep well that night, though. Our new brother snored like crazy. Stanley and I spent half of the night rolling him back on his side to shut him up.

Chapter Thirteen

Tic-Tac-Toe

On the day Little Paul's personal nightmare started, he had only been with us for just over a week. We were all playing tic-tac-toe in the yard. Paul wasn't very good at it. In fact, his co-ordination was crap. He had us all in stitches, as he attempted and failed to hop from one leg to the other. We were all light-heartedly teasing him. However, Stanley ended up changing the tone a bit and started calling him 'spazz' and 'a dumb shit'.

Paul was a self-conscious and feisty boy, who didn't take too kindly to Stanley calling him 'a spazz'. He quickly retaliated by chasing Stanley around the yard and threatening to beat him up. Stanley was too slippery for him though, and in his frustration at not being able to catch him, Little Paul spat at him instead. Then all hell broke out. They started fighting and things got very loud. So loud, in fact, they woke Roy up, who was working nights that week and usually slept throughout most of the day.

We, the older kids, knew it was more than our lives were worth to wake him up. That was why, whenever he was on nights at the weekends, we were dumped outside from when we got up in the morning to until he got up, irrespective of the weather conditions.

Roy came rushing outside effing and jeffing, as usual. He was definitely not happy and demanded to know what was going on!

Once Stanley had told him that Little Paul had spat at him, Roy went absolutely berserk. He grabbed hold of Little Paul and literally threw him through the back door.

"The rest of you bastards get in the effing house," he shouted.

At this point, I would normally have been shit scared of the beating that was about to be bestowed upon us. On that day, however, after seeing little Paul fly through the air and bounce off the side of the door frame as he went through it, I was more afraid for him. Roy had never done that to any of us. It was scary to witness.

Once inside, we were again ordered to assume the position of facing the wall with our pants down.

Stanley, Ella and I all obliged. Paul on the other hand simply crossed his arms in defiance.

"No," he said.

That was it. Roy flew into another rage, well and truly losing it. He punched Little Paul in the side of the head, sending him to the floor like a sack of spuds falling from a great height. Amazingly, Little Paul didn't cry or show any emotion. He just lay there on the floor, holding his face and glaring defiantly at Roy. God knows what was going through Little Paul's mind. *Does he have a death wish?* I wondered.

"You fucking little bastard, how dare you say no to me. Get the fuck out of my sight before I kill you, you little fucker," Roy bellowed at him. I remember those words so vividly and, as you read on, you will understand why.

Little Paul ignored Roy, just sitting there glaring at him, never even blinking an eye.

"No," he repeated. Roy laughed aloud, almost insanely.

"So, you think you're a big man, hey? We'll see about that, you little bastard boy," he yelled. He then ordered the rest of us to our beds. Needless to say, none of us hung around. That happened at half-past eleven on a Saturday morning. We weren't allowed out of our rooms until half-past seven the following Monday, when it was time to get ready for school. We weren't fed a thing all weekend, either.

Shortly after Stanley and I got into bed, we could hear sounds coming from downstairs, sounds that have haunted me for the whole of my life. I don't think I shall ever forget the way Little Paul squealed like a hundred pigs trapped in an inferno, as Roy beat him relentlessly for what seemed like hours.

All I could hear between each bout of squealing was Little Paul repeating the word 'no'. He was a feisty little boy and very stubborn!

Little Paul was finally allowed to crawl into bed in the early hours of the morning, so badly battered and bruised that he couldn't go to school for a week.

Even though Stanley and I were still wide awake, there was no bedtime chatter that night. The only person to speak was Stanley, who simply told Little Paul that he was sorry.

Fifteen years later, I spoke to Stanley about that night, and he told me that he still felt bad about starting the fight that day. Like me, he still had dreams of getting revenge on Roy for what he did to Little Paul.

If he could, he would have taken the beating for Little Paul. But that would have been fruitless, because far worse was to come for Little Paul.

I don't know what it was about Little Paul, what made him choose the path of defiance, to choose a beating rather than compliance. All I knew then was that, with Roy, he was playing a losing game and that he would pay a severe price.

Chapter Fourteen

The Coal Bunker

Little Paul challenged Roy repeatedly and continued to pay an increasingly heavy price. He was beaten so badly and so often; he spent more time off school than at school. The worst thing about it was that those people who should have noticed his absence from school, and investigated it, didn't. Consequently, Roy was free to do as he pleased.

Then, one day when Stanley and I arrived home from school, we found Little Paul locked in the concrete coal bunker at the bottom of the yard. He was completely naked and freezing. We spoke to him through the gap in the door.

He told us that Roy had beaten him throughout the day because he had sworn at Mum. He also said that Roy had ripped his clothes off him and set fire to them in the yard, whilst telling Little Paul that he wasn't fit to wear clothes because he was a, 'fucking animal'.

This happened in the middle of January, and Roy kept Little Paul in the coal bunker until gone 10 o'clock at night. I remember hearing the News at Ten come on the TV, just before Little Paul limped, naked and bruised, into the bedroom to collapse on his bed without saying a word.

It went on like this for months, with Little Paul spending more and more time in the coal bunker. Our dog Rex had a better life than he did. At least Rex was well-fed and taken out for walks. We never went anywhere apart from school. Little Paul didn't even get that respite. Stanley and I used to feed Little Paul bits of food and sweets through the gap in the door whenever we could.

That was until spiteful Ella told Roy of our antics. One day Roy caught us slipping an Arrow bar through the gap and gave us a beating with the belt. Ella was a sly, selfish bitch and definitely had a bit of Roy in her! That day Stanley and I sent Ella to Coventry. Personally, I haven't spoken to her since, and never will.

Little Paul regularly went without food. Roy used to tease him when he fed Rex the dog, asking, "Do you want some, you fucking little animal?" He would often put some dog food in a dish and put it in the bunker for Little Paul, laughing as he did so, thinking it was funny.

If we were watching, which we were sometimes made to do, 'to learn from it', according to Roy, he would start to laugh and look in our direction, expecting us to join in his sick joke. Acting as if it funny was his way of justifying his actions, in his sadistic fucked up way.

One night, when Roy went to release Little Paul from his cold, coal bunker dungeon, he noticed that the dog food had actually gone. When Little Paul admitted to eating it, Roy went berserk, dragged Little Paul into the house and beat the shit out of him again.

Chapter Fifteen

Little Paul's First Christmas

The Christmas of 1969 is a memorable one, but not because we all received lots of presents, played games, ate well and generally had fun, like most of the families in our street.

We, the boys, all woke up at about 5 o'clock in the morning. For once, Little Paul had been allowed to sleep in his bed for more than a week. We were excited at the thought of receiving a pressie or two and, more importantly, a chocolate selection box, which we usually had to share between the two of us.

Even though we had been awake for hours, we were not allowed downstairs until Roy and my mum got up, which wasn't until half-past eleven that day.

After being given the go-ahead, we all rushed downstairs and headed for the front room, where the pressies were usually laid out in piles. The piles were not large by any stretch of the imagination. There was usually one main present for each of us and a few stocking fillers, such as colouring books and pencils, socks and undies, plus the ever-popular selection boxes.

I found my pile and frantically started to rip them open. As I was doing so, I became aware of Little Paul standing in the middle of the room. I looked around and noticed that there didn't seem to be a pile for him. I knew that this could not be right, as I remembered that his old foster parents had dropped quite a few presents off for him only the week before.

Little Paul looked at Roy and asked him where his presents were.

Roy replied that animals don't get presents and that Paul was lucky to be here at all.

I'll never forget the look of total dejection on Little Paul's face, which was absolutely heart-breaking to see. Feeling awful for him, I gave him one of my presents to open. He took the present from me and launched it at Roy, calling him a bastard as he did so.

Roy flew across the room and knocked him out cold, before dragging him by the ankle out to the coal bunker.

When Roy came back into the front room he was ranting and raving about how ungrateful we all were, and that none of us deserved anything at all. He then sent us all to our rooms. It was twenty to twelve. Our Christmas had lasted the whole of ten minutes.

We never did get to open our presents; Roy threw the toys and selection boxes in the bin and unwrapped the clothing items himself.

Two hours later, the smell of roast turkey filled the air of our bedroom, as Roy and my mum sat down to eat their Christmas dinner. We got nothing!

That afternoon, I looked through my bedroom window onto the street. It was full of our friends and neighbours wearing their new clothes, riding their new bikes and showing off their new toys.

Why has my mum put me in this situation? I wondered. *I bet Caren and Duncan are having a great Christmas.* I also remember thinking that, no matter how long I lived, I would never forgive her selfishness. I never did and neither did I go to her funeral.

Even though it was the middle of winter and as cold as hell, Roy kept Little Paul in that bunker all night, with just a single smelly blanket to keep him warm. I remember letting him out the following day — he was almost blue with cold. I was heart

breaking to see.

He only managed to stay indoors for about four hours before getting on Roy's bad side once

again, ending up by being thrown back into the coal
bunker.

Chapter Sixteen

Paula to the Rescue

After a few months of life alone in the coal bunker, mostly naked and cold, the inevitable happened. Little Paul started to display signs of mild insanity. He started chanting, 'I'm not an animal, let me out. I'm not an animal, let me out'. He would continue chanting the same words from the time he was thrown into the bunker in the morning to well into the evening, when he was finally released with a slap to the head.

Occasionally, Roy would drag him out and give him a beating for it. But Little Paul would just start chanting as soon as the padlock was back on. It was horrible for us siblings having to play out in the yard and listen to Little Paul go slowly mad, whilst not being able to do anything about it. That would be more than our lives were worth.

I felt incredibly guilty then, and still do on an almost daily basis. Some of you reading this book will question why we didn't just tell someone in authority, a teacher or the school nurse? Without being there, you would never be able to understand just how terrified we all were for each other. We all felt that telling on Roy or my mum could probably lead to Roy killing one or all of us.

One day, our neighbour Paula had heard enough of Paul's chanting, and Roy's abuse of him. She waited until we were all out and climbed over the wall into our backyard. She then broke the padlock and released Paul from the bunker. Taking him into her house, she bathed, clothed and fed him.

Why didn't she take Little Paul to the police or Social Services? you're probably asking yourself.

Well, that's an easy one to answer. Roy was so well known for his violence that virtually everyone in the street was shit scared of him. Paula probably thought that Roy might take it out on her family.

That day, Stanley, Ella and I arrived home from school to find the coal bunker empty and the broken padlock on the floor. We began to get concerned for Little Paul's well-being. We knew he wasn't in the house, because Stanley and I had been upstairs to get changed and hadn't seen him. Personally, I thought that Roy might have gone too far with a beating, and had either hospitalised Paul, or even killed him. Ella and Stanley stupidly thought that he might have escaped and gone on the run.

We never mentioned the fact that Little Paul was missing, instead playing dumb and going to our bedrooms to play.

When Roy got home from work, he didn't notice the lack of chanting from Paul either, so he was unaware that Little Paul had gone.

That is, until Paula came around and knocked on our front door, with Little Paul in tow. She confronted Roy about his cruelty, and they had a great big row, ending in Paula threatening him with the police if she ever saw Paul in the coal bunker again. Roy threatened that, if she did, he would, 'burn the fucking lot of her family alive'.

Roy then told her to fuck off, grabbed Paul by the throat, pulling him inside, and slammed the door in Paula's face. Although Roy was obviously enraged by this confrontation, he didn't take it out on Little Paul, or us, there and then, which was unusual. He simply told Little Paul calmly to take off the clothes Paula had given him and put on some of his own.

Little Paul, to everyone's disbelief, refused. Roy didn't argue, he simply ripped the clothes off his back before sending us all to bed. *Another night without food.*

This happened at half-past three in the afternoon. Although Roy didn't issue any beatings right then, we all knew it wasn't over. He now had all afternoon to smoke dope and stew over Paula's intervention. Meanwhile, we waited in our bedrooms in fear of Little Paul's life.

At about 5 o'clock, my mum arrived home and Roy started ranting and raving at her about how her effing so-called friend had the effing cheek and the balls to confront him at his own front door.

The discussion grew heated, as Mum tried to explain that, by putting Little Paul outside, he was asking for trouble. Roy disagreed, accused her of siding with her friend and gave her a good beating. Then, he went to the pub for some rage juice (beer).

Roy arrived back home at about 11 o'clock and, because he had gone to the pub earlier than normal, he was drunker than usual, too. As soon as he walked through the door, he started to rant. It was almost as if he'd been practising it outside before entering. I can't remember it word for word, but it went something like, 'Where is that fucking bastard of an animal? Little Paul, get your effing backside down here!'

I looked over at Little Paul. He was awake and had heard Roy, but chose to ignore him, staying right where he was. Roy called a further couple of times. I don't know if it was fear or just defiance, but Little Paul still never moved, but just laid there, eyes wide open but vacant, almost resigned.

I often wonder what he was thinking that night, when he decided to wind up an extremely pissed off and pissed up Roy. Sadly, though, I never got to ask him. Now, I think I know why – it was probably just to piss Roy off.

Eventually, Roy kicked open the bedroom door, almost taking it off its hinges. He then dragged Little Paul out of bed by one of his legs and dragged him down the stairs. I remember hearing the bump, bump, bump of what I imagined was Paul's head bouncing off each step on the way down to his personal appointment in hell.

Within a minute or two of Little Paul's head hitting the last rung of the stairs, I heard the, now very familiar, sound of leather connecting with bare flesh. There was something different about this beating though — I never heard a single sound out of Little Paul, no defiant backchat, no squealing. Nothing.

I remember thinking at the time, *he's either dead, has become immune to the pain, or knows that not screaming out would piss Roy off even more.*

I suspect it was the latter, and that Little Paul knew that Roy got off on the begging and squealing. Sometimes when Little Paul used to squeal, Roy used to laugh aloud. He lashed out, laughing louder each time that Little Paul squealed.

Little Paul never came back to bed that night, and the following morning was nowhere to be seen. I looked outside to see that the coal bunker was empty. I wanted to ask where he was, but was afraid to. I feared that Roy had hurt him so badly that he was dead, or something. I was truly worried about him.

After breakfast, which comprised of cornflakes and hot water, as mum only had enough milk left for Roy's breakfast, I went to the under-stair cloakroom to get my coat for school. As I did so, out of the corner of my eye I spotted Little Paul, tied up, gagged and shaking from cold. He was lying in the foetal position and had brown coloured dried blood on his face and arms, as well as huge welt marks all over his body. My heart sank to my feet, my head filling with rage when I saw what Roy had done to my little stepbrother. I wanted to go upstairs and beat him to death. I didn't, of course. I was far too small and afraid.

"You ok?" I whispered, trying to hold back the tears. He nodded, he looked so defeated lying there naked and hog-tied. I remember thinking, *one day when I'm big enough, I'll kill that bastard for doing this!*

The under-stair cupboard was to be Little Paul's new dungeon. He spent most of the rest of his short life either tied up in the cupboard, or having the crap beaten out of him.

I hated having to witness Little Paul being driven to the edge of insanity, and have always felt guilty about the fact that I wasn't strong enough physically or mentally to stop it. I used to have dreams of killing Roy, one of which I remember one quite vividly.

We used to have a problem with rats back in the 'sixties. Virtually every household in our street had rat poison to hand, as indeed we did.

In my dream, I laced Roy's Friday night curry with some of the rat poison, whilst my mum was seeing to Lara. He would get Little Paul out of the cupboard to abuse him some more, by making Little Paul watch him eat whilst the boy went hungry. Roy teased Paul by saying how lovely his food was, and asked him if he wanted any. Little Paul just ignored him and stared him defiantly straight in the eye.

After he finished his dinner, Roy went to the larder, then produced and opened a tin of Chappie (dog food). He chopped it up in a bowl and ordered Paul to eat it. Paul, of course, refused. Roy was about to ram Paul's face in the dog food, when he suddenly grabbed his own throat and started gasping for air.

Paul then started to laugh insanely, whilst eating the dog food as if he was eating popcorn and watching a funny movie. Eventually, Roy would collapse like a big, black heap of shit on the kitchen floor. Then, men in white coats would come and take away Little Paul, who was still laughing as he went.

Obviously, I never poisoned Roy. Not because I didn't want to, I was just too afraid he would survive and kill us all. Unfortunately, the evil bastard is still alive today.

For weeks at a time, that dark, dingy, cold and lonely under stair cupboard was Little Paul's prison. Yet strangely, it was also his sanctuary in a way. At least Roy couldn't beat him whilst he was in there. The cupboard was so small that a man the size of Roy could not reach in to beat him. Little Paul knew this, and would often tuck himself into the deepest corner, making it frustratingly difficult for Roy to even get him out for a beating.

Unfortunately, Roy would always find a way, and the longer it took, the more severe the beating. To Roy, Little Paul was no more than a punch puppet, which he played with far too often.

On one occasion, Little Paul started to chant and repeatedly bash his head against the cupboard wall, while Roy was trying to watch the cricket on the TV. Roy got annoyed with the noise. Then, frustrated at being unable to drag Little Paul out to give him a good beating, he actually started to throw burning pieces of twisted-up newspaper into the cupboard, threatening to burn Little Paul alive. Paul eventually came out for his beating, then was thrown back in for the night, this time bound and gagged.

This was hard for us children to watch. Whenever we could, we would hold back food, or steal biscuits and pass them to Paul when we got our coats in the morning. It was tough watching a fellow child gradually being starved and losing his mind.

Occasionally, I would wake up during the early hours of the morning and sneak downstairs, steal a few biscuits and feed them to him and sit with him for a while, in the dark and in silence. I don't know whether it helped him or not, but it did ease my conscience a little.

Once, I did this and fell asleep. When Roy got up at 5 a.m. for his 6 - 2 shift, he found me lying there fast asleep. He woke me up and, surprisingly, calmly told me to go back to bed.

Later that day, when he got home from work, he took me to one side and said that if I did it again, he would beat me, too, and put me in the cupboard with Little Paul. To my eternal regret, I obeyed his order and didn't do it again.

Eventually, Roy must have got bored with battering Little Paul, either that or the authorities must have started asking questions about his non-existent school attendance. Whatever the reason, the regular beatings stopped. Roy gave him his clothes back and let him join the rest of the family. He also allowed him to sleep in his bed.

About three weeks into this new regime, I woke up in the early hours to discover that Little Paul was once again missing from his bed. I woke Stanley up and together we made our way downstairs, but found the under-stair cupboard empty. Confused, we then made our way into the kitchen.

What Stanley and I saw that night still makes me feel gut-wrenchingly sick – Little Paul kneeling stark naked on the floor, scooping dog food into his mouth. Even though he knew we were there, he never stopped until the bowl was empty. Stanley and I just guided him back to bed, none of us saying a word. What could we say?

Chapter Seventeen

The Day My Mum Turned into Roy

One day, when Stanley and I arrived home from school, there was a police car parked outside our house. We both suggested a possible reason for it being there. Stanley thought that Paula, or someone else, had reported Roy's abuse and that the police had come to arrest him. I thought that Roy had probably gone over the top with Little Paul and killed him.

Unfortunately, they weren't there for Roy at all. They had actually brought my step-sister, Ella, back from the C&C supermarket, where she had been caught shoplifting. Apparently, she had been caught trying to steal packets of biscuits.

As we entered the house, the bobby was relaying the details of Ella's misdemeanour to Mum. He also informed Ella that the shop had decided to take no further action on this occasion. However, she was now banned from entering the store and, if she was caught in there again, she would be taken to court.

Unbelievably, during the whole of this visit, Little Paul was hog-tied, naked, and stuffed in the under-stair cupboard. The entire time, I wanted to shout out, 'he's in the cupboard, he's in the cupboard!' I didn't, though, as I was too scared of the possible consequences. Instead, I hoped and prayed that Little Paul would start to bang his head against the cupboard wall, or start chanting as he usually did, but he didn't. He actually slept through the entire episode. After the police left, Mum became furious with Ella, beginning to eff and jeff at her, finally saying the seven words we dreaded and feared the most.

Once we had eaten tea, which consisted of boiled rice and cheap tinned beans in tomato sauce, we all sat down to watch a bit of TV. When Ella came into the room to join us, Mum told her that she should be in her bedroom, and that she wasn't allowed to watch TV. Actually, it went more like, 'you're not watching TV, you thieving little bitch. Bugger off to your bedroom'.

Ella, being a stroppy twelve-year-old, refused to leave, reminding Mum that she wasn't her mother and didn't have the right to tell her what to do.

On hearing this, Mum got up from her chair and landed six or seven full-blown slaps across Ella's face. She ordered her to stand in front of the gas fire until she was ready to apologise, calling her a horrible, thieving little cow. The gas fire, by the way, was on high. Mum then retrieved Roy's old leather belt from the coat hook in the hallway and warned Ella that, if she moved, she would leather the daylights out of her.

Initially, Ella stood there in defiance, but ten minutes or so later, she started to writhe in pain as the heat from the fire started to blister the back of her legs. She tried to rub her legs to protect them from the heat, but every time she did so, Mum whacked her with the belt.

After twenty minutes or so, I could see that Ella was in agony and I that blisters were forming on the back of her calves. Plasma started to ooze out. The smell was starting to get to me, too.

I remember looking over at my mum and noticing for the first time that her face had changed. No longer was it the gentle, soft and kind looking face of my mother. It was a harsh, witch-like, vengeful face. I recall thinking that she was changing, and not for the better. Roy was rubbing off on her!

Eventually, Ella gave in and said that she was sorry, and asked if she could move. Mum contemplated her request in silence for at least another two minutes before agreeing, and sending Ella limping to bed.

I think my mum must have realised that she had gone over the top, punishing Ella in that way, because she never mentioned a word about the shoplifting to Roy. If she had, then Roy would have wanted to beat Ella himself, but would have seen what Mum had done to her, and probably beat Mum up, too.

The following day we all went to school as normal, Ella wearing her thick black tights to hide her blistered legs.

That afternoon, as Stanley and I approached the house on the way home, we once again saw a police car parked outside. Wondering what the police were there for this time, Stanley and I continued to walk towards the house. We had just reached the front gate, when my mum came out with a couple of policemen and was clearly about to leave with them.

"What's up, Mum?" I asked her.

"It's nothing to worry about. I'll be home soon. Your Dad is on his way home from work. In the meantime, I want you to stay with Paula," she replied, as one of the policemen guided her into the back of his police car and drove off.

When we got indoors, we found Paula talking to another woman that I presumed was from Social Services, judging by the type of questions she was asking.

"What's up? Why have the policemen taken Mum away?" I asked Paula. Paula said she didn't know, but that Roy would be home soon and I would have to ask him.

I later found out via the newspapers and school gossip, that Ella had gone to school and told her teacher about the previous night's cruelty, also showing her injuries. The school must have called Social Services who, in turn, called the police.

My Mum and Ella came home from the police station well after the News at Ten had finished. I heard Ella come up the stairs and get into bed. After a few minutes, I heard the, now very familiar sound, of Roy beating the crap out of Mum. Judging from what he said between blows, he was more pissed off that Mum hadn't left Ella to him. Because of her stupidity, they were now under the watchful eye of Social Services. It seemed like he couldn't care less for Ella's welfare.

Once again, Little Paul had actually been in the cupboard throughout the whole day – even while the police were there to question and arrest Mum. He was also there all the time that Paula was looking after us at her house. Nobody noticed that Little Paul was absent. Out of sight, out of mind, I think the saying goes.

The following morning, Roy let Little Paul out of the under-stair cupboard, gave him some clothes and was actually nice to him for a little while. He was even able to go to school after about a week or so.

For the next few months, Roy's attitude to punishment was almost unbelievable. The belt never left Roy's waist, and when Little Paul misbehaved, he didn't get beaten, stripped and thrown into the cupboard. He was just sent to bed hungry, like the rest of us. Obviously, the close shave with the law had put the willies up Roy!

Chapter Eighteen

Mum's Day in Court

It took about three or four months for my mum's case to be heard before the Chester Crown Court. Her trial only lasted a day. She was found guilty of child cruelty, or something like that. I still don't know exactly what the charge was. All I do know is, that when Stanley and I arrived home from school that day, we were greeted by loads of Roy and Mum's so-called friends. They were both black and white, some were seated on the front wall, swilling down cans of lager or bottles of Babycham. There were twice as many more inside. They were drinking in celebration of Mum's two-year jail sentence being **SUSPENDED**.

How sick is that? I remember thinking. Most self-respecting adults would have been appalled at my mother's behaviour and outraged about the courts' leniency.

I don't know how she managed to stay out of jail, but regrettably, she did.

The most appalling aspect of the fucked-up situation was that the social services system of the early 1970's never removed the rest of the evil bitch's kids, not even Ella, whom she'd abused. The system was totally ineffective at providing child protection. Forty years on, and they are often still as inept!

Later that week, on the following Thursday, the story of my mum's court case was reported in the local newspaper. There was a picture of a bunch of people standing outside our house drinking. The headline went something like, 'Sickening abuser celebrates her freedom after only receiving a suspended sentence for dreadful child abuse'.

The following day at school, all our friends suddenly became distant and didn't invite Stanley and I to play football anymore. It was as if they felt sorry for us, but didn't know what to say, so they fell silent and avoided us. It didn't last long, though. The following week we were all friends again. There was a saying back then, 'today's news is tomorrow's chip wrapper'. It was true, because Social Services certainly forgot about us.

Four weeks after her court case, my mum and Roy finally got married. Yet again, on our return from school, we were met by a bunch of pissed-up adults sitting on our front wall and in our house. We kids were sent upstairs to our rooms and, once again, went hungry, while they played music and celebrated well into the early hours of the morning.

It soon turned out that their wedding was a sham, though, as I caught Roy with another woman. On one occasion, I was walking home from the youth club on a Wednesday night, probably about two weeks after Roy and my mum were married. Another time, I actually caught him kissing the same woman in his car. I tapped on the car window. Roy looked sheepish, as he wound down the window. He smiled, as if nothing had happened. Then, he gave me 10p hush money for a bag of chips

He hadn't needed to give me hush money. I wouldn't have told my mum. I knew that, if I did, she would start a fight with him and, inevitably, he'd beat the crap out of her. Me as well, probably, for grassing on him.

Eventually, some ten years later, he left my mum for the same woman that I'd seen him kissing in the car that night. They moved to Milton Keynes. He divorced her, too, five years later. Luckily, she was too old to have any kids.

Chapter Nineteen

Brigs Avenue. New House, New Start.

When I was eleven, about six months after Mum and Roy got married, it was time for us to move again. Our new house was slightly better than the one in Burley Street. It had two quite large gardens, one to the front and one to the rear. We kids thought this wonderful – we had grass for the first time ever.

We could also play to our hearts' content and not worry about getting told off for waking Roy up if he was on nights. Plus, it was the first time we had actually had grass or flowers. Grass was much better to play footie on than concrete.

The joy didn't last long, though. One day, a few months after we moved in, Roy got us three boys, Stanley, Little Paul and I, to dig up the back garden, so that he could 'grow some veg'. Reluctantly, we did as we were told. I remember it being hard work and taking us all weekend. Once done, he gave us each 10p, for 'working so hard'. He then promptly banned us from using it for playing in. He declared it a 'vegetable plot', even though he never planted a single seed there. He only ever planted stuff in the greenhouse, with its padlocked door, blacked out windows and God knows how many paraffin heaters.

I didn't know it then, of course, but I now suspect that he was trying to cultivate his own stash of Marijuana. He did smoke quite a lot of it!

One of the biggest downsides to the new house was that it also had an under-stair cupboard. It only took a week or so before Little Paul was once again battered, tied up, and flung into it naked, as a punishment for biting the boy next door. Who, by the way, was a lying scumbag of a racist, and who got a good kicking from me a few days later at school.

Chapter Twenty

New School and More Racism

The house move happened at about the same time as Stanley and I started going to secondary school. It was there that the racism really started to rear its ugly head.

At first, it was ignorant curiosity, with questions like, 'If he's your brother, why is he brown?' They called me a 'nigger lover', and named my stepbrother, Stanley, the 'Caramac Kid', after a particular bar of tan coloured chocolate.

I hated being treated differently just because I had a black brother. The teachers were not interested and turned a blind eye to the racial abuse. If Stanley or I complained, they would always turn it around on us, saying things like, 'don't be so sensitive', or, 'they're only joking, where's your sense of humour?' We stopped complaining and I dealt with the racist kids the only way I knew, by beating the crap out of them. It wasn't long before I gained a reputation of being the hard man and someone not to be messed with. Those who attacked my stepbrother also got it from me.

The kids I could deal with. The adults, on the other hand, were quite another thing altogether. They were so shallow and fucked up that they didn't even know they were doing it. Quite a few of the teachers used to look down their noses at us, especially the P.E. teacher, Mr F, who used to occasionally collect the free school meal tickets at lunchtime.

The kids who paid for their dinners were issued green or yellow tickets on alternate days. However, the kids who got free school dinners were always issued red tickets.

When this particular teacher was on collection duty, he would send all the red ticket holders to the back, saying stuff like, 'those that pay should get the first choice. Those with free tickets should be grateful'.

I hated Mr F in particular, because he always seemed to have a gripe with Stanley. One day, we were in the gym playing badminton when he started to rip into Stanley for some unknown reason. I don't know why, but I suddenly became angry with him for treating my brother like shit. So, with a full swing of my badminton racquet, I whacked the teacher right across his arse a couple of times. It sent the class wild with laughter, and embarrassed the shit out of him.

I was sent home, and when I told Roy what had happened, he didn't punish me as I'd expected. He just said that it was a good thing to stand up for each other, but warned me not to do it again. The following day I was given six of the best by the headmaster, which stung like hell. It was definitely worth it, I thought. Mr F never picked on us again. In fact, he left the school a few months later.

I remember that, on another occasion, when a school friend of Stanley and mine was having a birthday party at his house in Ruskin Road. He invited the pair of us to join him. However, there was no official invite card. We both went out and bought him a present and a birthday card, and made our way to his house.

When we rang the doorbell, his mum answered the door. She looked Stanley up and down before asking me what we wanted.

"We've come for John's birthday party," I said, as we both simultaneously handed over our presents and cards.

"Oh," she said, with a fake half-smile on her face, which had 'racist' written all over it.

"I didn't know you had been invited, and the house is already full, so I'm afraid you won't be able to come in, but I'll give John your cards," she said. With a smug smile on her racist face, she turned, went in and shut the door in our faces.

That was probably the day I wrongly started to feel real embarrassment at having mixed race brothers and sisters. I felt resentment towards my mother for putting me in that position. I felt so frustrated at the thought that, for the rest of my life, I would have to pay the price for my mother's selfish act in getting with a bloody black man.

Another time I remember quite vividly, was when Roy took us all to one of his relative's houses in Sheffield for a 60th birthday celebration.

Roy dropped me off at the shop just down the road from my uncle's house and told me to get him some cigs, which you could get away with doing back in the early 70s. I got the cigs and made my way to Uncle's house.

When I got there a black guy that I had never met before opened the door.

"What you doing here, boy?" he asked, with a stupid, quizzical look on his face.

"My dad's in there. I'm here for the party," I replied, annoyed at being called boy. I hated being called boy, by anyone, especially people I didn't know.

"There are no white men at this party, boy," he said, with another stupid, confused look on his wrinkled, black face.

"He's black," I replied, in a pissed-off, up yours manner.

He looked at me, kissed his teeth and shouted into the house.

"Does anyone have a honky boy wit dem?"

Fucking honky? Who do you think you fucking are? I thought.

Roy came to the door

"It's okay, he's with me. Don't ever call him a fucking honky again," he said, grabbing the guy by the throat. I simply smiled at the twat, as I followed Roy into the house.

That day, I learned that blacks could be racist, too. In fact, I would say from experience, they can be more racist than white folk!

Chapter Twenty-One

My First Girlfriend

At the age of twelve and a half, I met my first girlfriend at the local youth club disco. Her name was Gillian, and she was drop dead gorgeous, and quite tall, too. I was definitely punching above my weight.

By the time I had been going out with her for about four weeks, things were going really well. I'd even been around to her house a few times and, met her family, who all seemed very nice.

Then, one night my brother Stanley came along to the disco with me. I introduced Gillian and her friend to Stanley, and we all seemed to get on really well together. In fact, the night went so well that my brother ended up going out with Gillian's girlfriend.

The following day, when I went around to Gillian's house after school to take her for a walk, her dad answered the door. He wasn't his usual smiley self. In fact, he was scowling.

Sensing he wasn't too pleased to see me, I used my politest voice ever.

"Hi, is Gillian there, and can she come out for a walk?"

"No, she's not here, and furthermore, she is not allowed to see you again. I don't want you coming around here, either," her dad replied, pointing to the gate with a very stern look about him, as if to confirm his wish that I leave. I was confused as to what I had done.

"Why?" I asked, but he turned on his heel and went back inside, shutting the door in my face. I felt a right idiot.

All the way home I asked myself what had I done to upset her, or her dad for that matter. He had seemed completely cool with Gillian and I the week before.

Then, just as I was hanging my coat up in the under-stair cupboard, from the corner of my eye I saw Little Paul, naked and tied. Then it clicked. It was a racist thing.

It was two weeks before I managed to speak to Gillian in person. When I did, I wished I hadn't. She had told her mum that I had a mixed-race brother and that my dad was black. Her mum told her dad and, next thing you know, he's demanding that she never see me again. I had been right; racism had reared its ugly head again.

I kept my family situation well and truly secret from my next girlfriend Mary, for as long as I could. However, after a whole year of going out with her and only spending time either out, or at her house, and her whining on about meeting them, I relented. I finally took her home to meet the Obeah Man. She didn't seem to have a problem with the black side of my family. Nor did her parents, which was refreshing.

Then, one day, a few weeks into her starting to come to our house, Mary and I were about to leave to go back to hers, when Roy told me to tell Little Paul he could come out from the under-stair cupboard. I surreptitiously opened the cupboard door and told Paul that he was allowed out. Then I left, with one very confused girlfriend in tow.

Needless to say, I never saw or heard from her again after that. I don't blame her.

Chapter Twenty-Two

Angela: And Then There Were Seven!

Not long after my last girlfriend dumped me, I learned that Roy had yet another daughter, who went by the name of Angela, Ella's sister. Apparently, she was only six weeks old when her mother died in the fire.

She had been fostered by a German couple since she was seven weeks old, and had remained with them for more than ten years.

Need I say that Roy had never mentioned her, and never intended to mention her to my mum? Then, one day, out of the blue, he received information regarding a request from the German couple about permanently adopting her.

Roy didn't like that idea. Suddenly, he wanted Angela back and applied for her to be returned to him. To cut a long story short, he won the custody battle and the right to get Angela back!

However, the German couple had built a loving bond with Angela and were not keen to let her go. They were also very astute people. They insisted that all the children should meet on several occasions before a complete return took place.

That's how it came about that, for the following six weeks, all of us, except Little Paul, were taken to their house on a Sunday afternoon for tea. There we would play with Angela and her foster sister and brother.

From the first Sunday afternoon visit, I realised just how the perfect family lived, and just how poor our family was. The contrast was stark. Better food, better clothes and definitely a cleaner and tidier house. The German kids' toys were also superior to ours. It was quite a treat for us all. I remember wishing that they would adopt me.

I recall on one occasion, the German mother asking Roy where Little Paul was. Roy simply lied to her face, saying that he was visiting his uncle. The truth was that Little Paul was in the under-stair cupboard, and had been for days. He had been badly bruised by Roy, for biting another kid at school and being suspended. There was no way he would be allowed to visit the German family's house, for fear that they might report his injuries to the police, or give them ammunition that could be used to overturn the judge's decision about the adoption.

After six weeks of Sunday visits, it was finally time for Angela to move in.

One Friday, when we all arrived home from school, we found the breakfast bar covered in food. I knew instantly that Angela was on her way. *Poor kid,* I remember thinking.

She was duly delivered by the German mother at half-past five that evening. The mother wasn't allowed in. Mum simply took Angela's case from her, said thanks and shut the door. Now that Angela had finally arrived, we were all allowed to tuck into the buffet.

Angela had lived a totally different life to us, so our little council house and having to share a room with three others was obviously a shock to her system. I could tell. She looked shocked and deflated, as she watched the rest of us eagerly tuck into the grub. Even Little Paul, with his battered and bruised face, had been let out for the occasion.

It didn't take more than twenty minutes for Angela to get on the wrong side of my mother.

Mum had noticed that Angela wasn't tucking into the buffet, and asked her if she was not feeling good. Angela replied that she was fine. However, the look on her face said something different, almost as if she were looking down on us.

"Why aren't you eating the food?" Mum asked her.

"I don't eat white bread, just brown, and I don't like the other stuff, either," answered Angela, her arms crossed defensively.

I looked straight at my mother for her response. Her face went bright red, her false smile turning into a fearful mask of annoyance and anger.

"You do now, or you'll starve, you stuck up little bitch. Now eat the fucking sandwiches, or I'll tell your father when he comes home," Mum replied. *Uh oh, that's not a good idea, Angela. You need to toe the line, or become Roy's new punch puppet,* I thought to myself. I hoped that Mum's annoyance didn't result in us all being sent to bed, especially with all the food on offer. Thankfully, it didn't.

It wasn't that Angela was rude, but she had just become accustomed to different, finer foods. I think she regretted joining her new family from the first minute she entered the House of Pain.

About a month or so after Angela moved in, the school started calling my mum to tell her that Angela was self-harming and tearing her clothes.

At first, Roy accepted her behaviour as part of a settling-in phase, which she would get over. However, another couple of weeks later, Angela absconded from school and went around to the German couple's house, pleading to be allowed back.

They called Roy and suggested that Angela stay the night at their house, promising to drop her off first thing the next morning. Roy went ballistic over the phone, telling them to have her ready by the time he got there, or there would be trouble.

Roy didn't like the attention Angela was bringing on the house. Nor was he too pleased at the German couple meddling in his business. Luckily for Roy, he hadn't hit Angela for several days, so there was no evidence of physical abuse for her foster parents to use against him.

Roy was clever. He probably knew that Angela might try to go back to them, or that they might check up on her at school. So, he used to slap Angela across the lower legs, so that her long, white socks would hide any marks.

That night, when he and Angela arrived back home, we were all sent to our rooms. Not long after, we heard Mum and Roy start arguing. This was followed by the, ever-familiar, sound of my mother begging him to stop beating her. He always beat her, or us, when things didn't go right for him.

At the same time, Little Paul's mental health was beginning to be questioned at school. It was suggested that Little Paul should see a therapist. Roy couldn't risk Paul spilling the beans, so he took him out of school for good, telling the authorities that he was going to spend some time with his aunt and uncle in Milton Keynes. Unfortunately, they fell for his lies, thus giving Roy plenty of opportunities to carry on abusing him.

Chapter Twenty-Three

Time to Get Out of Here

Just after my 16th birthday, I left school and went to work on the railway as an apprentice signalman. That was just a posh title for a signal box runner, someone who ran, or rode from the station to the various signal boxes carrying messages. It was okay during the day, when I could see where I was going, but the night shifts were horrendous. Running to and from the different signal boxes in the pitch dark was dangerous. God knows how many times I fell onto the tracks. Needless to say, I didn't stay there for long.

I then got a job as an apprentice cutter at a well-known, upmarket clothing manufacturer, one who made suits for Prince Philip and Prince Charles, as well as for other wealthy celebrities.

After I had been there for about a year, I managed to save enough money for a deposit on a flat just off Nantwich Road. It wasn't much to look at, and only had one room and a bathroom. But to me, having my own place was heaven. I didn't have much in the way of possessions, nor was I left with a great deal of spending money after my rent and bills were paid, but I couldn't have been happier to be free of the House of Hell. I would like to say that I was free of Roy too. Unfortunately, that wasn't the case.

A month after moving in, I stupidly left my key with my mum one day. My landlord had arranged for a local gas fitter to fit a coin meter in the flat. As I was at work all day, I couldn't be there to let the fitter in, so I asked my mum to pop round and do it. Not long after the meter was fitted, I fell sick at work and was sent home for the day. As I approached my flat from an adjacent street, I saw Roy and a woman leaving it.

I waited until they were out of sight and headed indoors. I knew he'd been there, and probably for some time. There were two still-wet glasses on the drainer. I also checked the pedal bin and found several empty beer cans. No prizes for guessing what they'd been up to.

The following Saturday, my day off, I arranged for the Yale lock to the flat to be changed. I told Roy and my mum that someone had broken in and that the landlord had changed the locks. I never gave my keys out again.

Eight months later, I was made redundant from work and ended up on the dole. Now unable to keep up with the rent, I had to give the flat up and ended up moving back in with the Obeah man. I slept on the sofa in the front room for the next three months. During that time, I applied for, and then waited to join, the army.

I finally left Roy, Mum and my siblings behind on the May 5th, 1980, when I joined my new family, the Para's.

I have never been back to that house since, and do not intend to have any form of relationship with anyone from those first sixteen years of my life. Not even with my siblings.

In September 1981, I received a letter from Little Paul telling me that he'd had to have his right arm and shoulder amputated because of cancer — the very same shoulder that had smashed into the back doorframe on the day when Roy had hurled him through it.

Inside the envelope was a picture of Paul without his right arm and shoulder. In his left hand was a tiny, black puppy. Apparently, Roy had bought for him.

I remember looking at the picture and feeling sick to my stomach about the fact that the only time Roy had ever been kind to Little Paul was when he was dying.

To my own disgust, I never replied to Paul's letter, which is something I will regret for the rest of my life. I rejected him at a time when he probably needed me most.

A year later, just after I got back from the Falklands conflict, I was informed by my Commanding

Officer that Paul had died at the age of nineteen. The cancer had spread throughout his body.

Personally, I think it was Roy's constant battering and abuse that led to Little Paul contracting the cancer that ultimately killed him.

I did go to Little Paul's funeral, but incognito. I watched from a distance as they laid my little stepbrother to rest.

In West Indian culture, it is customary for the relatives of the deceased to fill in the grave after the service. I watched, as Roy vigorously filled Paul's grave, whilst over-doing the distraught father bit.

Me, I think he was just glad to be able to get rid of the evidence of his horrendous cruelty.

Roy was a sick and evil man, who should have never have been allowed around children, or women for that matter.

You may have noticed that, apart from their births, Jane and Lara, my half-sisters, are hardly mentioned in this story. That is because Roy, for some reason, never laid a finger on them. At least, not while I was there.

Postscript

I decided to write this mini-book as a mark of respect for Little Paul. I believe his story should be told. While I can't remember all the abuse he suffered at the hands of our demonic parents, I believe I have given you a taste of what cruelty he and the rest of us kids suffered during the 1960s and 1980s. I also hope that the organisations and people that should have looked after him, like Social Services and the Law Courts, will now understand just how badly they let Little Paul, and the rest of us, down. More importantly, I want them, and future generations of social workers and judges, to learn from our horrible experiences — and their mistakes!

Thank you for taking the time to read this.

Other books by P T Saunders

Me and My Black Dog: Complex PTSD:

A truly disturbing story about a Falklands/SAS veteran's battle with PTSD, and his eye-opening stay on a psychiatric ward.

By joining the army in 1980, I managed to escape the clutches of a disgustingly evil man. However, I didn't realise that I was jumping from the proverbial psychological frying pan into the fire.

During more than twelve years of service in the armed forces, I was engaged in the Falklands war, the first Gulf war and carried out several tours of Northern Ireland. I also spent three years of my career serving with the Special Air Service.

The traumatic events that I experienced during the above conflicts, and those I both experienced and witnessed as a child, have had, and continue to have, a major impact on my mental well-being.

In this book, I try to explain how, over the years, my life has been blighted by these traumatic events and how that affects my life today.

And

Left Behind: A gripping psychological thriller you won't be able to put down.

Made in the USA
Middletown, DE
05 February 2022

60582320R00116